SPEECH

OF

HON. J. COLLAMER, OF VERMONT,

ON

SLAVERY IN THE TERRITORIES.

DELIVERED IN THE SENATE OF THE UNITED STATES, MARCH 8, 1860.

The Senate having resumed the consideration of the following resolutions, submitted by Mr. BROWN on the 18th of January:

Resolved, That the Territories are the common property of all the States, and that it is the privilege of the citizens of all the States to go into the Territories with every kind or description of property recognized by the Constitution of the United States and held under the laws of any of the States, and that it is the constitutional duty of the law-making power, wherever lodged, and by whomsoever exercised, whether by the Congress or the Territorial Legislature, to enact such laws as may be found necessary for the adequate and sufficient protection of such property.

Resolved, That the Committee on Territories be instructed to insert, in any bill they may report for the organization of new Territories, a clause declaring it to be the duty of the Territorial Legislature to enact adequate and sufficient laws for the protection of all kinds of property, as above described, within the limits of the Territory, and that, upon its failure or refusal to do so, it is the admitted duty of Congress to interpose and pass such laws.

The question is on the amendment of Mr. WILKINSON, to strike out all after the word "resolved," where it first occurs, and insert the following:

That the Territories are the common property of the *people* of the United States; that Congress has full power and authority to pass all laws necessary and proper for the government of such Territories; and that, in the exercise of such power, it is the duty of Congress so to legislate in relation to slavery therein that the interests of free labor may be encouraged and protected in such Territories.

Resolved, That the Committee on Territories be instructed to insert in any bill they may report for the organization of new Territories a clause declaring that there shall be neither slavery nor involuntary servitude in such Territories, except in punishment for crime whereof the party has been duly convicted.

Mr. COLLAMER. Mr. President, the resolutions under consideration relate to the condition of slavery in the Territories, and propose to provide legislation in relation to that subject, especially legislation to protect and preserve it there. The discussion on this subject, as it was begun and has gone on in the Senate during the progress of this session, has taken a very wide range. I have no fault to find with that; but it seems to me, after all, that we might bring ourselves a little nearer to some practical application of principles. When we consider the condition of our country—I mean of our whole country—the condition of society which exists in it, and the adaptation of our measures to that condition of society, we may bring ourselves to the practical application of some important principles.

Now, what is the state of society here? Take our nation, for which we legislate, the whole of which is a proper subject of our consideration, the whole of which is to be considered in measuring out our different degrees of policy, and the measures calculated to advance its interests. No legislation can be valuable, unless upon the whole it is an advantage to the country for which it is made, and we must consider the actual condition of that country at the time, in order to see the practical application of the measures we are about to pursue.

We have, it seems, Mr. President, two conditions of society existing in this country—that existing in the slaveholding States and that existing in the non-slaveholding States, which I, for brevity, shall call, as they are usually called, the free States. The condition of society in the free States, which include, in round numbers, about

Printed by Lemuel Towers, at $1 50 per hundred copies.

/ 5 3

two-thirds of the inhabitants of this country, is based on this idea, that all men are to be educated; that there is to be universal suffrage; that men are to be educated with a view to discharge this duty and privilege of suffrage. When our fathers at the East entered upon this experiment at first in New England, all the notions which had existed for ages in other regions of the world, in relation to landlord and tenant, lord and vassal, patrician and plebian, master and slave, were entirely to be obliterated, and all the notions which had prevailed, too, of primogeniture and of entail, and everything that was calculated to perpetuate those distinctions in society, were to be done away with. In short, they proposed, and the idea they entertained was, to enter upon an experiment of a free and equal system of republican government; that every man should own the land he cultivates, and every man should cultivate the land he owns; that there should be none to rule and none to serve; that every man should serve himself, and then he of course would have a faithful servant.

That system is not merely ideal. It practically prevails through the large body of the free States—not so much in the cities, not so entirely in the more densely populated regions; but such is the actual condition of the landholding part of the people of the free States. I will not spend time to elaborate this system any more. I do not propose now, or at any other time in the course of my remarks, to say anything to commend it particularly to the acceptance of any one. I simply wish to state it, and briefly to describe it, and there rest in relation to that.

The other condition of society, existing in the slaveholding States of this Union, I would rather cite as described by another, than undertake to do it myself. Mr. Calhoun, in 1837, said:

> "Many in the South once believed that it (slavery) was a moral and political evil; that folly and delusion are gone. We see it now in its true light, and regard it as a most safe and stable basis for free institutions in the world. * * * The southern States are an aggregate, in fact, of communities, not of individuals. Every plantation is a little community, with the master at its head, who concentrates in himself the united interests of capital and labor, of which he is the common representative. The small communities aggregated make the State, in all whose action, labor and capital are equally represented and perfectly harmonized."

I am not about to make any remarks in relation to the question of whether this is a desirable or undesirable condition. I simply desire briefly to elaborate a little what Mr. Calhoun here says of it. From these remarks, two things are quite obvious. In the first place, it is obvious that is an aristocracy. He says that these communities, of which the master or owner is the head, aggregated, make the State, and the owner is the representative of these separate communities. That meets my idea of nothing more nor less than an aristocracy. I do not say that this condition of things is censurable. I do not use the word "aristocracy" in any bad sense. I say it is simply that. Another thing, which is perhaps but an ingredient of the first, is, that the mass of the community—I do not speak now of the slaves—are, in effect, practically ignored. The masters representing, as Mr. Calhoun says, these separate communities, make the State, and, as the representatives of the labor and property of which they are masters and owners, they of course guide the State, and hence, he says, there comes to be no collision. We all understand that a large majority of the southern people are not slaveholders, and they never will be probably. Of course, according to his own statement, they are essentially left out of the account.

These two conditions of society, inasmuch as they are both in existence in our country, and no doubt will be during our lives, and probably for centuries to come, present to us a problem to solve; and the question is, what is our duty here, for this body is the representative of these two interests. I regard it as the duty of Congress, so far as the powers which have been delegated to it will enable it to do, to endeavor to promote and advance the prosperity of all parts of this country; of both these sections, if you call them sections; of both these conditions of society. That may be a very difficult problem; but the more difficult it is, the more we should be willing to grasp it, meet it, do our duty in relation to it. I think we are not at liberty to set aside any one part of our country, or any one of these conditions of society, on the ground that we cannot exactly reconcile its privileges, its interests, its duties, with those of the other. That problem is put into our hands in the formation of our Government, in the existence of this Government, and we cannot do our duty if we avoid it.

It is, I say, Mr. President, not an easy task to shape the policy of this Government, to order the forms of our commercial intercourse, to lay our duties and taxes, to frame all our laws in such a manner as shall best promote the advantage of the whole of this people, and both of these classes, and this whole community. It may be true, at times, that we shall find the interests of one part conflicting in some degree with the interests of another part, and therefore it is that the problem may be difficult of solution, practically in our hands; but it is nevertheless the problem put into our hands. It is to that we must address ourselves. It is that we must perform as far as we can, and as much as in us lies.

The first thing that occurs to my mind is this question: is it at all probable that we can, either of us, induce the other to adopt our system of society? Argue it as long as we please, spend as much of our time and breath about it as we may, in commendation of the respective system which we represent, and to which we belong, after all, I believe there is very little reason to suppose that in this Hall one party will be able to induce the other to adopt its system. It is not very likely, it is not very probable. Whenever the system of either party is attacked, and its weaknesses attempted to be exposed, each may stand on the defensive, and that is well enough, if so be that it is conducted in appropriate spirit, and with that courtesy and urbanity which should become the places that we occupy in this, which ought to be regarded as an august body.

It will hardly do to say that these two conditions of society cannot exist in the same nation. There is a coexistence in the same nation. There is another kind of coexistence in the same municipal government. They are not the same thing. I fancy that, after an experiment of eighty years or more, we may at least say that they can exist, and prosperously, too, in the same nation. The lesson of our own experience teaches as much as that these two conditions can exist, and exist prosperously, in the same nation. But when we say that, we should recollect that the word "nation," as applied to a people like ours, is a term composed of an aggregate of separate nations, in one sense separate sovereignties; and all the internal and municipal regulations to which the condition of society belongs, fall appropriately and exclusively within the jurisdiction of the local authorities of the Sovereign States.

Then there may be a well-shaped and well-conducted and prosperously-conducted nation, with one condition of society, in one State, in one municipality, and another in another State. They may both be prosperous within the same nation; but, after all, they cannot coexist in the same municipal government. That is a mere truism, perhaps. It requires one simply to state it to apprehend it. I say a State cannot be a non-slaveholding State and a slaveholding State at the same time; and I may say, I may add with equal truth, that I think our experience shows us that, under a territorial government, a Territory cannot be at the same time a slaveholding and a free Territory. I believe that experiment has been attempted, and it is a failure; the thing cannot be. It would seem to be very obvious on the mere statement. It would involve a paradox.

Well, now, sir, what shall we do with this country, having these two conditions of society spread over it and existing in it? What is our duty in relation to the matter? We have no quarrel or difficulty in relation to slavery, so far as it exists within the separate States. It exists under the operation and protection of the governments of those separate States, peaceably and quietly. But the question arises, what shall we do in relation to it when we come to the territory which lies out of and beyond the jurisdiction of the several States? We must keep the peace about it; it must be arranged in some way. What can we do with it? How can we get along with it, quietly and peaceably? I think we, like any other people, might be enabled, if we were so inclined, to draw some lessons of advantage from our own experience, and from the history of our own country. We are apt to forget, in the hurry of new and untried experiments, that after all, experience is the safest guide for to-day and the safest guide for truth. We speak of our fathers—they who established this Government. How did they manage it? Is it not well enough for us occasionally to look at the old way, and ascertain how it was? The further we get into difficulty, the more troubles we experience in trying new modes and new experiments, the more we ought to be inclined to see how this matter was managed originally, and how that management succeeded. How was it? I think nothing can be more clear, on a candid examination, than that they looked upon slavery as a great evil. So admits Mr. Calhoun himself; undoubtedly it was true. No man disputes that now. How did they propose to manage it? It was in this way: the old Congress of the Confederation was sitting at the time the convention was sitting in Philadelphia. In that Confederation Congress they acted in relation to the then known and then owned territory of the United States, lying out of and beyond the limits of the separate States; and, in providing a Government for it, enacted that slavery or involuntary servitude, except for crime, should not there exist; it was entirely forbidden. That provision was handed over and duly notified to the convention that was sitting to form the Constitution; sitting cotemporaneously. They understood that, and it was in no way disapproved by them. They provided in the Constitution that Congress should have power "to make all needful rules and regulations" for the disposition of the territory and other property of the United States; thus bestowing on the new proposed Government the power of control over the Territories, and they immediately exercised it in the First Congress, by legitimating and adapting the provisions of the ordinance of 1787 to the then existing form of government.

There was another thing. They did not look upon slavery then as a mere local matter—a matter of mere local interest. The *nation* provided for the Northwest Territory; but that was not all. It was then undoubtedly the general prevailing opinion that if they cut off the supply of slaves by prohibiting the African slave trade, and limited the extent of territory in which slavery should exist, by confining it to its then existing limits, it would finally die out. There is no doubt that they entered upon that experiment. They vested in Congress the power, after 1808, to which time the extreme southern States then desired to continue the trade, to cut off that foreign supply—to cut off the African slave trade; and they had in the ordinance of 1787, the continuance of which the new Constitution contemplated, a provision for limiting the extent of territory in which it should prevail.

I have been charged over and over—I can remember at least three times, by three different gentlemen in the Senate, in the progress of this discussion—with having said, which was true, that I believed the more limited the extent of territory to which slavery was confined, the sooner it would come to an end. The honorable Senator from Alabama, (Mr. Clay,) the honorable Senator from North Carolina, (Mr. Clingman,) and, I believe, other gentlemen, have seemed to think that, in approving of that sentiment, I am an Abolitionist; and one Senator says that is nothing more nor less than a plan to smoke them out—not a very elegant expression. Have I entertained any new thought on that subject? I desire to call attention for one moment to a single remark made by the Senator from Virginia at this session. Mr. Mason said, on the 23d of January, speaking of those who made the Constitution:

> "I believe this was their opinion: their prejudice was aimed against the foreign slave trade, the African slave trade, and their belief was, that by cutting that off, slavery would die out of itself, without any act of abolition. I attempted at one time to show, by the recorded opinions of Mr. Madison, that the famous ordinance of 1787, so far as it prohibited slavery in the territory northwest of the Ohio, was aimed at the African slave trade, and aimed at that alone; the idea being that if they could restrict the area into which slavery could be introduced from abroad, they would, to that extent, prevent the importation of slaves; and that, when it was altogether prevented, the condition of slavery would die out of itself; but they were not Abolitionists, far less within the meaning and spirit of the Abolitionist of the present day."

That is the view I wished to present, in shorter words. They entertained the idea that if the nation would cut off the foreign supply, and would limit the area into which slavery was to go, it would die out. I am not now proposing to say how far this idea of theirs was correct; but I must say that I have a strong desire to play out that play. Let us go on and carry through the experiment on which this Government was founded; because it was under this idea—in the meridian blaze of this idea—that our Constitution was framed. It was framed by men who entertained this thought, and it was framed for the purpose of carrying it out. Hence it was that the power to cut off the foreign supply was vested in Congress, and the limitation in the Territories was done in the ordinance approved by Congress.

Mr. President, is there anything new in the idea which now constitutes the leading feature of the Republican platform—that is, keeping slavery out of the Territories, and keeping the foreign supply still cut off? One would suppose, who had come into this body for the last two or three months, that somehow or other this sentiment, this principle, this proposed object, was a new and unheard of aggression that was utterly unexampled; that there was no precedent for it in the Government; that it called upon all men, everywhere, to raise their voices in utter execration of the whole of it; and we have been called upon, from day to day, instead of proposing to carry out this principle, to disband utterly, throw down our arms, and disperse, as the English said to our fathers upon the field of Lexington. Sir, there is nothing new in it at all. It was the very framework, it constituted the great especial element of the Constitution; it was one of the great leading purposes of its formation. Gentlemen have wandered so far and so fast from this principle, amid the variety of dogmas now set up, one of them being parent to the other, they have made so large a departure, that when they come to look at the thing in its modern aspect, men are startled at it, because it does violence to their newly-invented dogmas, not because there is anything new or strange in it.

But, Mr. President, we acquired other and further territory than what was owned at the time the Constitution was formed. We did not at that time, if you please, properly own that part of the country which now makes Mississippi and Alabama. It belonged to Georgia. Our people claimed it—claimed that the title to a large part of it, at least, was in the United States, and not in Georgia. That was not merely the part ceded by South Carolina. There was another small piece; which was, the difference of the line of Florida as made by the British treaty, and as practically run. How did the United States arrange the matter when they acquired more territory—that part which they got from North Carolina which makes Tennessee, and that part which they obtained from France—the Louisiana purchase? How did they manage under this same Constitution in relation to the subject of slavery in that country? I had occasion to examine, with some care, this very question some time since, and I presented it in as brief words as I could in the report which I made in 1856, in relation to the Kansas difficulties. As I said then, I desire to inquire what our Government did in relation to that, for two purposes: in the first place, to show what power they exercised, and then the manner of exercising it. I think the manner in which they exercised it will clearly show us what power they understood themselves to possess; and not only so, but the manner in which they executed that power, so as to show us clearly their purposes.

What did they do? I grant to the Senator from Georgia, for I believe he has called our attention two or three times this session to the act of 1798, that it is not true that Congress always prohibited slavery in the Territories; not that they had not the power to do it, but because of its inexpediency. The true ground on which they went, the rule they followed, was this, as the whole lesson of our history will show, where slavery was actually existing in the country to any considerable or general extent, it was, though somewhat modified in Mississippi and Orleans Territories, suffered to remain. The fact that it had been taken there and existed there was deemed an indication of its adaptation and local utility. Where slavery did not in fact exist to any appreciable extent, it was by Congress expressly prohibited, so that in either case, the country settled up without any difficulty or doubt as to the character of its institutions. In no instance was this difficult or disturbing question left to the people who might settle in the Territories, to be there an everlasting bone of contention as long as the territorial government existed. It was regarded as a subject in which the whole country had an interest, and therefore improper for local legislation.

To illustrate this, I will not go on with the history of governmental action from time to time, as Congress made different territorial governments in the country northwest of the Ohio. I need not show how they continued to repeat over and over again the utter prohibition of slavery; but I will call attention to the act which has been remarked upon by the Senator from Georgia, in relation to Mississippi. As to Tennessee, we all know that North Carolina, in making the cession of the territory to the United States, prohibited them from doing anything tending to the abolition of slavery. In relation to Mississippi, I do not understand the action of Congress exactly as the gentleman from Georgia presents it. The truth is, that the United States claimed a large part of that country, now forming Alabama and Mississippi, and Georgia claimed nearly the whole of it. When the Mississippi territorial act was passed, in 1798, it was formed in anticipation of, and it appointed a way of fixing commissioners for, the settlement of that dispute with Georgia. The territory was settled, as far as it was settled, with slaveholders and slaves. It was expected that Georgia, in making her cession, would do as North Carolina had done in relation to Tennessee. That territorial act of 1798 remained unexecuted until 1802. In 1802, the commissioners of Georgia made settlement with the United States, and then the United States agreed to pay Georgia $1,250,000, for which she quit-claimed all her right, claim, and title, with certain reservations; and, amongst other things, she put in a clause forbidding the extension of the anti-slavery clause of the ordinance of 1787 over that territory. They made their grant on that condition.

What does that show? The Senator from Georgia says:

> "In 1798, when Congress legislated in relation to Mississippi Territory, they did not prohibit slavery."

No, sir, it was already there; actually established, and it was expected that Georgia would insist on keeping it there, and she did insist on keeping it there.

But that was not all. The United States then, in that very act, prohibited the importation of slaves from abroad, though they could not prohibit it in the rest of the United States until 1808. By what power did Congress do that? Certainly they received no power for it from the provision of the Constitution that "the migration or importation of such persons as any of the States now existing shall think proper to admit shall not be prohibited by Congress prior to the year 1808." That did not give them any power about it except to prohibit it in all the States after 1808; but they did proceed to prohibit the introduction of slaves into the Mississippi Territory in 1798. Why? Simply for the same reason that they did the rest: they considered themselves as possessing the power, in framing territorial governments, to frame them in such a way, and with such prohibitions and conditions, as they thought would best promote the interests of the nation. They derived the power, no doubt, at that time, from that clause of the Constitution called the territorial clause, by which they were empowered to make all needful rules and regulations for the Territories. None other can be found. There cannot be found a clause in the Constitution which gave them the power, unless it was that. I know that it is said, with regard to Louisiana and other acquisitions obtained by treaty with foreign nations, inasmuch as they have power to acquire, they have the necessarily incidental power to govern; but that cannot apply to Mississippi. It was not acquired by treaty from a foreign nation at all. They exercised the power there under the territorial clause.

Again, when our country made the Louisiana purchase from France, in the first act forming the territorial government of Orleans Territory, now Louisiana, which was in 1803 or 1804, Congress did not prohibit slavery; because it was already there, and because it was adapted to the country, I suppose they thought. They suffered it, but they did not leave it so. They provided that no slaves should go in there except in families for settlement; and in the next place, they provided that no slave should be taken in there in any way that had been imported into the United States after 1798. Why 1798? In 1798 they passed that Mississippi act prohibiting the importation of slaves from abroad into Mississippi. They soon learned that it afforded very little security to keep out imported slaves from Mississippi, when they could be imported into Georgia and taken over into Mississippi. Congress, therefore, provided, in the act for Orleans Territory, that no slave should be taken in there in any way, in families or in any other way, that had been imported after 1798. Now, I would ask, did not the people of South Carolina, or Georgia, or any other slaveholding State—and a great many of them were such at that time—own their slaves which they had imported from Africa in 1800, and 1801, and 1802, and 1803, just as they owned any other slaves they held? If any of them were property, were not those slaves property? Clearly they were. Well, then, how did Congress have a right to prohibit their taking them into Louisiana? They did exercise the power, and no man doubted it. It remained for fifty years, and no man questioned it.

It is unnecessary, in order to show what was the power, as then understood by them, that they should, on all occasions, have prohibited slavery entirely. The fact that they did not do that does not show that they had not the power to do it. No, Mr. President, a power to regulate is a power to prohibit. Nothing is more fully settled, for instance, than that the power to regulate commerce is a power to prohibit commerce altogether, as was fully settled in relation to the embargo. Congress did regulate this matter in the Territories precisely as they pleased. If the cotemporaneous exposition, if the usages and practices, under the Government, by those who made it, and, immediately after its formation, continued and persisted in, uniform in its operation, can prove anything—and it seems to me the best possible proof, when any doubt exists as to the construction of a paper—then, I say, it is clear Congress had and exercised the power, both in the territory they owned at the time the Constitution was adopted, and in that which they acquired afterwards, either from any of the confederated States, or from a foreign country. They exercised this power of regulating, curtailing, or prohibiting, as they in their judgment believed to be best for the country.

Such is the lesson of our experience as to how this matter was originally settled. In the progress of affairs, and in thus arranging for the Territories and settling them peaceably, they brought up State after State in perfect peace and success and prosperity until, I believe, fourteen States had been admitted out of those Territories, one-half slave and one half free; they had grown up, under this patronage and this administration of the General Government, in the full exercise of this power. In the progress of this history a difficulty was found in relation to the State of Missouri. We had then a large tract of land utterly unsettled; the settlements in the Louisiana purchase had commenced near the mouth of the Mississippi, and gradually proceeded up; but a large part of the Territory was entirely a wilderness, and Congress found themselves in difficulty as to the question of slavery and freedom in that Territory. What did they do? It occurred to the mind at once, "it cannot be slaveholding and free territory at the same time; we cannot have it both at once." I can hardly conceive of any result that would more naturally occur to the mind than to divide it. If two men own a field, and one wants to sow it with oats and the other with wheat, and they cannot have oats and wheat together with any success, I do not know any other way to get along with it peaceably but to divide the field, and then it may be cultivated with mutual advantage. This is an old lesson; it began very early—I have had occasion before to call attention to it, and will again. "And Abraham said unto Lot, let there be no strife, I pray thee, between me and thee, and between my herdmen and thy herdmen, for we be brethren." "If thou wilt take the left hand, then I will go to the right; or if thou depart to the right hand, then I will go to the left."

This territory was divided; Missouri was admitted; the line of 36° 30′ was run, and it was declared that shall be our division. Was there anything wrong in that? Was there anything so extravagant and extraordinary in it that we should now go to war with our fathers who made peace among themselves by it? Is not their example worthy of imitation? It certainly is by all those who really desire peace; but if politicians and other men can make themselves capital out of a constant turmoil and trouble, I suppose they will never agree to it.

Now, Mr. President, what is the proposition of the Republican party? Nothing more, nothing less than to restore that line. I do not suppose that those who obliterated it will render any assistance to again drawing it upon the surface of the earth, but that is the proposition, and that is all there is to it; for if we say that slavery shall not go into the Territories, it amounts to that, for there are no Territories for slavery to go into, but what are arranged, as things now are, to any extent, unless it is north of that line. If we go no further than that, we simply say you shall take nothing by that vote that repealed it. That is all. Exclusion of slavery from the Territories, and leaving it uninterfered with in the States where it exists, as insisted on by the Republican platform, is, in my estimation, but practically restoring the Missouri compromise, and I shall so call it in my remarks.

There may be other aspects of the question; but really when we disembarrass it, strip it of its collaterals and contingencies, and present it in its practical light, there is all there is of it. Is it then one of those subjects that call so loudly on all parts of the country, and especially on the South, for expressions of execration of us? It seems to me not. There is not only nothing new in it, but there is nothing of the least apparent injustice in that which has been once fully agreed to, and I think never should have been disagreed to.

Mr. BENJAMIN. I will not interrupt the Senator from Vermont by a question, if it embarrasses him at all in the course of his argument; but I would ask him if he intends referring, in the course of his remarks, to which I am listening with great interest, to the fact that the whole South endeavored, by every possible means—by remonstrance, entreaty, and every other possible means—to get the gentlemen who now compose the Republican party to agree to just what that Senator says is what they now want?

Mr. COLLAMER. You mean to extend it to the Pacific?

Mr. BENJAMIN. Yes; to leave that line, not only as a sacred line, as established in 1820, but to extend it to the Pacific; and the proposition now is to put it back, after you have extended the free States south of that line.

Mr. COLLAMER. What do you mean by that? California?

Mr. BENJAMIN. You took possession of a Territory south of the line; and after you have got that, now you say, restore the line back again.

Mr. COLLAMER. If the gentleman will be a little patient, he will find that I shall not blink that point at all; but I do not understand it as he does. I have, however, no desire to avoid it. I expect to call attention to it. I said that, in my opinion, that line should not have been obliterated. I cannot here but remark, in the first place, as to the making of it. The gentleman from Virginia (Mr. HUNTER) in the course of this session spoke of that as being a northern aggression; and he made a discovery new to me, when he supposed the North made the line. The truth is the South made that line. I do not say that no northern men voted for it. There were a very few, enough, with the southern votes, to make a majority; but the great body, the majority, of its supporters were southern men. They made it.

I actually heard with astonishment the honorable Senator from Virginia put that down as one of the northern aggressions. That is a new discovery to me. To my mind, that is very much like the man of whom I heard during the Canadian difficulties, who said he was willing to go over there and help the Canadians to fight the British any time; and when asked why, he said, "the British are always pecking at somebody; at one time they came into Boston and threw all our tea into the harbor, and we have not got over that yet." (Laughter.) I think this is about as new a reading of history as that. But, sir, what purpose had that compromise line answered? What had the South got out of it? First, the making of that line admitted Missouri; it left Arkansas to be admitted south of it, and left all the country that could be formed into States anywhere south of 36° 30′ to be made slaveholding Territories, and so, of course, slaveholding States. In the next place the South wanted Texas; we know what for. Undisguised was the object. Mr. Calhoun officially, as Secretary, of State, announced to the world that it was to be obtained to perpetuate slavery. There was no disguise about that. They wanted that. How did they get it? One among the means by which they obtained it, was this: they provided that the line of 36° 30′ should be continued across Texas. I know it would not give much even if that had been kept. It did not amount to a great deal; but I shall have occasion to refer to that again. Whatever was north of that line in Texas, was sequestered to the cause of freedom. That was one of the elements that entered into the obtaining of the annexation of Texas. It was one of the means by which they effected that. Afterwards, there was a dispute growing out of what I thought there was never much ground for—a claim of Texas to a large quantity of land now forming part of New Mexico, and which was thus sequestered to the cause of freedom, if in Texas. The United States finally gave Texas $10,000,000 to quit-claim all her right to that territory and have it belong to New Mexico, where it would stand a chance of being slave territory, and would not fall within the saving of this clause of the Texas annexation resolutions.

It is not necessary to trace the history of the difficulties which were attempted to be settled, and in some measure were settled, by what were called the compromise measures of 1850; but the great point which was desired to be obtained by the action of that year—professedly desired, and I do not know but really—was that Congress should settle the subject of slavery for all the country we then owned, as the compromise line of 1820 had settled the condition of the country in relation to all we then owned, and the ordinance of 1787 as to all we then owned. How was it settled in 1850? It was said that if Congress passed the measures in relation to Utah and New Mexico, and the other compromise measures then agreed upon, there would be no territory left about which to quarrel in relation to the subject of slavery; it would all be settled and arranged, and there would be, as they said at that time, a finality of that topic. Those compromise measures were passed. They were passed because the Missouri compromise line had settled all the Louisiana purchase, and they took it up there and settled all beyond; and these two standing together made a perfect provision for the whole subject in the whole Union. Thus it was that the Missouri compromise line entered as a very large element into the formation of the compromise measures of 1850. It was the leading ingredient in it, because that settlement was in relation to a larger and more important part of the country than the other.

By means of this compromise line, the South had, from step to step, as I have stated, obtained these several advantages; and what do we come to next? This had operated as a sort of stool-pigeon, a decoy, to enable them to go on, step after step, with these various arrangements as they wanted. It quieted the North; it enabled them to obtain from the North these various measures. But, sir, when they had gotten them all through; when there was no more expectation of obtaining anything south of the line; when they had secured every advantage it was practicable to have from it, now they must just at once take down the stool-pigeon, destroy this decoy, obliterate the line, and spread their peculiar institution as much north of it as they could. That was attempted to be done in 1854, by the legislation of that year.

Now I come to the point that the Senator from Louisiana suggests. Why was that compromise repealed? Why was that line obliterated? Here let me say, that the more excuses a man makes for a thing, the less we are satisfied with it. A good excuse or reason is perfect in itself; it is not made by collecting together half a dozen imperfect ones; and I will now call attention to some of what are said to be the causes of that obliteration. First, we are told by the honorable Senator from Louisiana that the North were unfaithful to the agreement. I know the honorable

Senator from Louisiana, in putting the question to me, does not use those terms; but they are the terms that are attempted to be used in presenting this proposition to the community; that the North were unfaithful and untrue to that Missouri compromise line. How? What do you mean by being true and faithful to a compact? What is meant by it in the English language? I take it, it is the carrying out and executing the compact according to its terms, according to the understanding of it when it was made. What was the understanding in relation to that compromise line when it was made in 1820? It was to run through the French purchase—the Louisiana purchase, if you please—from the Mississippi river to the Rocky Mountains. Had not that always been carried out until it was repealed? What had ever the northern people done that was untrue to that compact? Nothing, nothing. Nothing is pretended. Then that pretended excuse is unfounded. The allegation that they had been untrue to it themselves is simply untrue.

But we are told that they would not vote to extend it after the Mexican war and our obtaining from Mexico territory towards the Pacific. It is said they would not consent to extend that same line through to the Pacific. In relation to that point, I say, first, it is no matter what their reason was; it is not true that there was any sort of obligation on them to make another bargain and extend it over other country. It never was any part of the original compact that it was to be extended over other territory; and therefore it is a matter of no sort of importance what their reason for their action was. I was not present at the time those gentlemen objected to that. I am not possessed of what their true reasons were. I do not think they needed any. When one man propose to another to enter into a compact, he has simply to say, "I do not intend to entertain it." What then? It is very obvious that the gentlemen who represented the free States on that occasion were in a very different condition about that territory, for the country obtained from Mexico had no slavery in it; it had been abolished while the country belonged to Mexico; it was not a slaveholding country at all; and therefore they probably may have thought, though I do not know it, that their constituents would not have approved of their making a bargain to give away and make into slave territory that which was already free, by any means. But gentlemen say they agreed to divide the new Territories that were slaveholding. Very well; you may have been generous on that occasion; that makes no demand on the other side to reciprocate it on a different occasion. But that is not the great difficulty with the thing. Suppose the North, as you say, would not agree to extend that line over the newly acquired territory: what then? You might find fault, if you pleased; perhaps you would have occasion to do so; I do not say whether you would or not; but this I say what sort of excuse can a man of common discernment make to another of similar character, to say, "Sir, because you will not make this other additional bargain, I will break up the one I made myself." That is what you did do. You repealed the Missouri compromise line in the country called the Louisiana purchase, for which it was made, and to which it was confined. To my mind this is rather a lame excuse; in short, it is no excuse at all; but it is said that that was the reason why it was repealed.

The next reason is the one which is put into the repealing bill. That bill, called the Kansas-Nebraska act, which repealed the eighth section of the Missouri act, does not say that it was repealed for any such cause as that which I have just noticed. It says that it was to be declared null and void; because it was inconsistent with the principles of the compromise acts of 1850. That is the reason given in the bill. I can merely say, that those who passed it put on the record that as the reason, and it is—I will not give it any bad name—a sort of equivocation for any man to resort to any other reason when he has recorded the one which he gave at the time; he is estopped from giving any others. That is an entirely different reason, and utterly inconsistent with the first; and, besides, they are both false; for the latter one, though it was put on record that it was inconsistent with the compromise of 1850, is just as wrong as the other. The fact is, that compromise of 1850 was made on the ground that the former one of 1820 was part and parcel of the arrangement; and therefore this excuse is equally unfounded with the other.

But, Mr. President, I have now attended to three reasons for the repeal. The gentleman from Virginia found fault with the compromise of 1820, because, he said, the North made it, and it was an aggression when it was made. The next reason that is given is, that they would not extend it. The third reason is the one put into the bill, that it was contrary to the compromise of 1850; but we have this session, and perhaps within a short period before, got another reason. It is said that it is unconstitutional; that Congress was well justified in repealing it, because it was unconstitutional.

Mr. WIGFALL. With the consent of the Senator, I will ask him a question. I do not want to protract this debate, because I have a little matter that I want to get up after it is over; but, just as a matter of curiosity, I should like to know what the Senator understands to have been the principle of the compromise of 1850 as to Utah and New Mexico?

Mr. COLLAMER. It was this: there had been difficulties and controversies about the forming of territorial governments in those Territories. Congress could not agree on it. At first we had California in with them——

Mr. WIGFALL. Leave California out.

Mr. COLLAMER. It was in it, and we cannot help it. It was in it for a year or two, until California formed a State government. Then, when it came to the compromise period of 1850, as part of the compromise, California was admitted as a State. As to Utah and New Mexico, there had been bills, especially for New Mexico, pending in Congress before that. Various measures had been proposed in relation to them; the northern people insisting on the application of the provision of the ordinance of 1787, declaring that slavery should never exist there. They would not pass them without it. When Congress passed them, they were passed without that, and with a provision that the people might make them free or slave States, and that they should be admitted as they should be formed, whenever they should become States.

Mr. WIGFALL. That was the principle?

Mr. COLLAMER. That was the provision in relation to them.

Mr. WIGFALL. That the Territories should settle it for themselves; and that Congress should not, in the meantime, interpose to prohibit the introduction of slavery?

Mr. COLLAMER. No, sir. When the gentleman says the Territories should settle it for themselves, he includes more than I understand it——

Mr. WIGFALL. I am not a squatter-sovereignty man.

Mr. COLLAMER. That is a point you have got in that was not put in. It was put in in relation to Nebraska and Kansas; but it was not put in in relation to the others.

Mr. WIGFALL. Did they not have the right to regulate their own affairs, without any interposition of Congress as to slavery?

Mr. COLLAMER. There was nothing said about that.

Mr. WIGFALL. Was there any interposition on the part of Congress, either to establish or prohibit slavery there?

Mr. COLLAMER. There was none.

Mr. WIGFALL. Then the principle, if there was any principle involved in the Utah and New Mexico bills, was, that Congress should not legislate either to establish or protect——

Mr. COLLAMER. You are drawing a conclusion.

Mr. WIGFALL. I am asking for information.

Mr. COLLAMER. The bills are very plain.

Mr. WIGFALL. These are historical facts; only philosophers can give reasons. I was asking for a reason, possibly; but I want the Senator, before he goes on, to answer that. You see I am a new Senator yet, and do not understand these questions. Now, I understand—at least before I got here I had supposed that the Utah and New Mexico bills left this question beyond all doubt—that Congress did not, in those bills, either interpose for or against slavery. Is that true, or is it not?

Mr. COLLAMER. I have stated about that. There had been a difficulty in forming those territorial governments, because a part of the country insisted on putting in the ordinance of 1787.

Mr. WIGFALL, Yes, sir.

Mr. COLLAMER. Congress could not agree to it; but when they had the making of the compromise of 1850, as part and parcel of it, these two Territories had territorial acts passed for them, which will speak for themselves, but they were passed without the prohibition of the ordinance of 1787.

Mr. WIGFALL. Precisely. Then I want to ask the Senator, when you come to form a new territorial bill as to Kansas and Nebraska, if you are not following out the precedent? I do not talk about the principle spoken of in the great speeches that were circulated in thousands and hundreds of thousands, but if the precedent was not followed when the Missouri restriction was repealed and the Kansas-Nebraska bill was passed, as the Utah and New Mexico bills were passed, without any provision either favoring or disfavoring slavery? That is the question.

Mr. COLLAMER. The gentleman has made his own speech, taking his own premises, and drawing his own conclusions. I can present very different views. I think that that whole compromise must be taken together.

Mr. WIGFALL. The omnibus was turned over, and they were passed as separate bills.

Mr. COLLAMER. They were passed as separate bills, but they all constituted a compromise, and are so spoken of in the Nebraska act. It was a compromise consisting of three or four acts passed here. That compromise put together made a whole, and I insist that it was a disintegration and destruction of the principle on which they went when you repealed the compromise line which settled the condition of a large part of the territory, and which settlement entered into and constituted part of the very compromise of 1850.

Mr. WIGFALL. With the permission of the Senator, I will again draw his attention to the fact that the Utah and New Mexico bills were passed without any provision either establishing or prohibiting slavery, and that the Kansas-Nebraska bill, in order to be passed in accordance with that precedent, must necessarily have repealed the Missouri restriction, or it would have recognized the right of Congress to interpose. Therefore, what the Senator would call non-interposition, I call interposition. What he would call non-intervention, I call intervention. As there had previously passed a bill in 1820——

Mr. COLLAMER. The gentleman is making a speech of his own; he has not asked me a question. He is making up his own logic, stating his premises, and drawing his conclusions in his own way. I say all the parts of that compromise constitute a whole. They should be left to stand together, and I have already explained what I considered entered into and constituted a part of it. Now gentlemen say, that when they came to pass a law making a territorial government for Kansas and Nebraska, they had to pass it like those for which they had a precedent. How was there any obligation to do that? Not the least in the world. If a man had sold land for ten dollars an acre, a large tract, and should afterwards sell a similar amount to the same purchaser for twenty dollars, could he then say, "now you must give me twenty dollars for the first?" They had made arrangements all about that line before; the compromise was made on that basis; and now, when they came to make a territorial government, were they obliged to make it on the basis of the Utah act, passed since the line was arranged?

I was stating the reasons which were attempted to be given for that repeal. The first, mentioned here by the Senator from Virginia, was that the North made it, and that it was an aggression; the second was that it was not extended over other Territories, but a new bargain made for them; the third was, that it was inconsistent with the compromise of 1850; and the fourth is, that it was unconstitutional all the while. To my mind, this last is pretty much like Jack Fallstaff's, "I knew you all the while." It is an after-thought, a new discovery. Is it possible that these gentlemen can give that as an excuse for doing the thing when they did not explain it or state it at the time they did it?

Again, is it becoming in these people to say, "We agreed to this proposition; we made this arrangement with you in 1820; we have had our States admitted south of the line, according to it; we have had the consideration on our part, and now we turn around on you, and tell you we never had any authority to make it, and we knew we had not when we did it; it was a great delusion from beginning to end?" The truth is, that, in common ethics, as well as in law, when a man exercises the power to do a thing, he is estopped from saying he had not the power. If a man sells me a horse as his, he cannot afterwards, after taking his pay, tell me that the horse belonged to another man. He has no right to say it; he is estopped from saying it. So with those who exercised this power. They are not at liberty, in law or in morality, to say that they had not the right to do it. It is totally immaterial whether they had or had not the power. With them, it should be held sacred; for they did it.

But, Mr. President, I have been unable to see what was the difficulty in this compromise line, making it constitutional. Was it unconstitutional because it was not long enough? Is it possible for you to say that if it had been extended to the Pacific it would have been a good and constitutional line? Here stands the honorable Senator from Louisiana; a more ingenious lawyer certainly can seldom be found, whatever may have been said about the Philadelphia lawyers; but he stands here and puts to me a question implying plainly that the difficulty was, we would not extend the line Then you were willing to extend it and forbid slavery north of it clear to the Pacific? Yes. Then how had you a right to do it; or do you mean to acknowledge that you were then trying to play another trick on us? I do not believe anything of this notion; you did not believe it at the time; and it is an excuse that should not be permitted to be made by any man.

But, Mr. President, how has the experiment of the repeal of the Missouri compromise, and the measures which followed it, worked? What was involved in it? What did it propose to do? If the honorable Senator from Texas (Mr. WIGFALL) were now here, and designed to obtain my idea on this subject, he would probably obtain it. The Kansas bill was entirely a different bill from the New Mexico and Utah acts. In that section repealing the Missouri compromise line, it not only declared that, being inconsistent with the principles of the compromise of 1850, that line was thereby declared inoperative and void, but it further went on to provide that Congress would neither legislate slavery into the Territory, nor exclude it therefrom; but that the people thereof should be left perfectly free to regulate their domestic institutions in their own way, subject only to the Constitution of the United States. Why did they put in that last clause? I am very apt to forget it, because I have always supposed that all laws made within this nation, whether by a State Legislature or by Congress, were subject to the Constitution as a matter of course. I did not suppose repeating that could alter the fact. Still, there was a stress laid on that. Some gentlemen have said in the Senate, "We did not think that the people were invested with power to regulate this institution in their own way, constitutionally;" and yet they voted for that bill, with that expression in it.

The honorable Senator from Virginia said, last session, that he did not believe Congress had power to invest the people of a Territory with the authority of legislating and settling its institutions in their own way under the Constitution; but he agreed to give it to them, subject to the Constitution—meaning, thereby, to leave it to the courts. That seems to me to be a very extraordinary mental reservation—to vote for a law which was, in the opinion of the voter, unconstitutional, in order to leave the question to the courts! Congress did invest the people of the Territory with that power, if they could, subject to the opinion of the courts, whether they could or not. I cannot but say, though it may be rather a harsh mode of illustrating it, that it is like the French infidel officer going into battle, and praying the Lord, if there was one, to save his soul, if he had any. (Laughter.) That is to say, "we give this power, if we have power to give it; but we do not believe we have any power to give it." That is your position.

That was a very different bill from the others, Utah and New Mexico. I know it has been said since, that really and in fact nothing was meant by all that rigmarole of words, except that when the people came to form a State constitution, they could make it a free or a slave State, as they pleased. Then, that action was very unnecessary. There is no doubt that, if gentlemen desire to make issues amongst themselves, that is a matter for their consideration. No man can mistake the expressions of that bill; and those expressions were not put in there for any such purpose as is now pretended by some; and I can tell you why. The very provision of the New Mexico and Utah act, wherein it was provided that they should be admitted either with or without slavery, as should be provided in the constitutions when they came to form a State—that very expression was already in the Kansas-Nebraska act, eight sections before the other words to which I have alluded. It was all provided for before you came to the repealing provision. That was not there, then, for any such purpose. It evidently does mean, as it provides, that the people there, while a Territory, and as a Territory, should settle the matter in their own way.

I will not now enter into the question whether they could or could not; but that was the power given. Were they left to form it in their own way? Certainly not. In the very beginning, in the choosing of the very first Territorial Legislature, more than four thousand men under arms from Missouri invaded and subjugated them, and made their election. They never were left free to act in their own way; and then followed all the extraordinary laws and means which were resorted to, and all the violence which resulted; this Government saying that it would not correct anything, and those laws should be carried into effect with the whole power of the Government; together with the ravages of war, and bloodshed, and burning, and desolation, which went over Kansas Territory. These all followed your act. Did you think they were worse than other people? What were you attempting to do? You were attempting to have a Territory that should be a slaveholding Territory and a free Territory at the same time; and you could not make it go through. In the nature of things it cannot. The people supposed their territorial government was to settle the question. The Missourians went over, and chose the territorial government, because they understood it was to settle it. All understood it so at that time. That was an entirely different thing from the New Mexico and Utah bills. That was a new experiment attempted.

How has it worked? Is anybody so much satisfied with the results and effects of that experiment that he desires to push it further? I do not believe there are many. The people of the North believe that was all wrong; in the first place, because it was contrary to the original policy of the Government. In the next place, they do not believe it is beneficial to the country to turn it over to the people, on the plains of Kansas, to fight out a subject of this kind in which the nation is interested. It never was tried before, and I trust will never be tried again.

But, Mr. President, it is said great danger will result from the action of the Republican party, if they should really apply their principles; if they should reëstablish the Missouri compromise line and stop the spread of slavery in the Territories, which the repeal of the line attempted to effect. We propose to do nothing more and nothing less than restore the Missouri compromise by excluding slavery from the Territories; and if we should carry it out, does not that make a pretty fair division of this country? We have, in round numbers, about one-third of our people in the slaveholding States. We have about two-thirds of them in the free States. We have about three million square miles, in round numbers. It does not differ a hundred thousand from that. It is very fully shown, from the best evidence and the best information, as collected and collated by Professor Henry, and to be found in the agricultural report, in 1856, that there is a little more than one-third of this whole country that is incapable of settlement. We may be unwilling to acknowledge that to ourselves; but that is the fact. As stated by the Senator from Georgia, and which I believe is true, the slaveholding States now have within their territory, (and they are in the occupancy of eight hundred and fifty thousand square miles,) almost one million, of the best part of the country. They are but about one-third of the people. There will be left, then, for the other two-thirds of the inhabitable part of our country, one million one hundred and fifty thousand square miles. Have they not much the larger part? Have they not got the best part? Can gentlemen say now, that, when we declare they shall be and ought to be confined to that, we are trying to smoke them out? It is the other side that is in trouble. The free people, with their institutions, according to numbers, are about to be restricted to less than their proportion of the country, and they are to be smoked out or starved out, if either.

What, then, should prevent us from doing this justice? What is there wrong in it? What is there unprecedented in it? What is there unjust in it? Certainly nothing. But still it will not do, they say, to have a Republican President chosen; it will be a cause of dissolution. Why? Because they say some of the free States have passed unfriendly laws to that provision of the Constitution about fugitives from labor. Mr. President, in relation to those laws, I would call gentlemen's attention to this: it certainly is the exclusive duty and obligation, as well as privilege, of every State to protect the liberties and lives and property of its own citizens. I say it is exclusively their duty within their own territory.

I not very unfrequently, especially among unlettered people, hear it asked, why Congress cannot abolish slavery? and I cannot but say that I think at times there have been some mistaken notions, like those suggested by the Senator from Texas, about this being a consolidated Government, and talk of that kind. Take the plainest case imaginable. Here is a man, if you please, in a northern State, confined by another as a laborer in his cellar, chained, for years. The whole power of the United States Government cannot affect it. They have no power to grant any relief. Just so in the southern States; no matter how many men they hold in bondage, if you call it such, it is a matter exclusively theirs; Congress has no power over it. If they, as some of them do, propose to reduce to bondage a large number of men who are free, no matter how we may look on it, it is utterly beyond the reach of the power of Congress. So, on the other hand, I take it, the right and duty to protect their own citizens in their liberties and lives is the exclusive duty and privilege of the States.

It is not true, as was properly suggested by the honorable Senator from Ohio (Mr. Wade) yesterday, that because the South have a right to pursue and take their slaves that run away, and bring them home, therefore every man in a free State is subject to being taken away. Let us think, for a few moments, of the decisions on that subject. In 1842, came the decision of the Prigg case. That case contained some pretty important things, new to the country at that time. We may have become familiarized with them now; but they called for the action of the States.

The Supreme Court decided in that case that the owner of a fugitive slave had the right to pursue him into a free State, without any process whatever, to take that slave, recapture him, and carry him home. I take it that it is the privilege and duty of every State to so arrange the manner in which a man exercises his rights, that the rights and privileges of others may be secure. That is a matter of legitimate legislation. We have, for instance, in the State in which I live, a considerable number of free colored citizens. I do not know their number now—a thousand, perhaps more. They are just as much entitled to the protection of the laws as the white men. When this opinion was pronounced by the Supreme Court, that a person could come there and take a man, claiming him as a fugitive slave, and carry him away without any process whatever—for the court said he might do it, if so be that he committed no illegal violence—was it not obvious that our colored population could be in no way safe, I do not say against honest and honorable slaveholders, but against all men who might come to claim them—slave dealers? They could not be safe, if there was to be no process, if no court was to pass upon it, if nobody was to interfere with it. If he was to exercise this right without any limitation, or without any arrangement or control, how could they be safe? It was very natural, and did happen, as the Senator from Georgia says, that in Vermont they began as early as 1844; yes, sir, two years after that decision. When they understood the decision, they did say, "Now, this will not do. We cannot have our people subjected to this sort of arrest. If these men have the power to arrest him; if they are entitled to a man as a slave, let there be due process; let there be given to our people some sort of security." Therefore they did provide that the taking of a slave without process should be unlawful—illegal. Was there anything extraordinary in that? Can you see in that nothing but enmity to that provision of the Constitution? Clearly, not at all.

That case further decided, too, that State magistrates might act under the law of 1793, if they pleased, not otherwise; but if the States forbade it, they could not. They decided another thing: that this subject of the reclaiming of fugitives from labor was peculiarly and exclusively the business of the General Government. They decided not only that the States had no right to interfere with it, but they said they had no right even to make a law to carry it into effect. I know that Judge Taney and Judge Daniel differ as to that; they dissented on that point; but all the rest of the court, I believe—unless, perhaps, Judge McLean, certainly Judge Story and a majority of the court—decided that all laws made by the States, tending to secure fugitives, were utterly null and void. Therefore the States were, by that decision, released from all obligations. They were not expected to do anything about it, friendly or unfriendly. It does not seem to me that there can be any good ground to complain in relation to the States not carrying into effect the fugitive slave law, or that provision of the Constitution, when they were distinctly and expressly told it was none of their business; and that all the laws they could pass about it, or in any way inconsistent with that provision of the Constitution, were simply and utterly void.

The legislation which was made on that occasion in my State provided for the security of our citizens by the act of 1844, of which the Senator from Georgia complains, though I do not understand from his note one thing. He says that our act denies to the district court of the United States power to entertain a *habeas corpus*. I do not know but that may be so; but it is out of my mind, and I think it is not the fact. But when our people said their sheriffs and justices should not interfere with it, and that our people should not be taken without process of law, they further provided that nothing in that act should be considered as extending to any person that was acting as a United States judge or marshal, or anybody acting under him. It is true that other legislation has since taken place. When, in 1850, the new fugitive slave law was made, it is true that was received in that quarter much as the Senator from Ohio says it was in his State. It was obnoxious, abhorrent; it was against the feeling of our people, and especially that part of it which required them to become aids and assistants in following and running after alleged fugitives, under heavy penalties.

It is said that this act was essentially the act of 1793. We did not view it so; we do not now. By this act, certain men called commissioners, who were appointed by the district courts, are clothed with certain powers. Those commissioners had existed before that. They existed by law, appointed by the courts for certain purposes. Those purposes were to take depositions, to bind over criminals, take bonds—in short, all the preparatory steps looking to a trial in some court. But they were mere ministerial officers, with no power of adjudication, no power of decision.

Under the law of 1793, in relation to fugitives from justice, all that is done is to return the man who is a fugitive from justice to some other State, for the purpose of taking his trial there. It looks to a trial. It is a mere preparatory step. But when you come to this law of 1850, to all practical purposes the commissioner is clothed with final power of adjudication, which is entirely a new feature.

I know justices might send a man out under the act of 1793, if they pleased to act; but that was all safe, as they were our own officers. So far as the courts, the district judges, or circuit judges, are clothed with authority, the acts of 1850 and 1793 are alike; but, as respects the powers with which the commissioners are clothed, they are utterly unlike. When an application is made to a commissioner, and a man is brought before him, said to be a fugitive from labor, he hears and decides the case. He sends him, if you please, from New England to Texas. I do not know but that a man might claim another as a fugitive from labor who was an apprentice. The very first man, if you please, of the State of Virginia or Georgia, might find some one coming and claiming his son as an apprentice, for service due in California; and the commissioner must send him there. You will observe, the commissioner does not, in this case, send back the man, as the fugitive from justice is sent, for the purpose of taking his trial in some court. He sends him definitely; it does not look to any court. It is not a ministerial act, preparatory to trial anywhere. It is not a step preparing him to be tried by any court. It is ultimate, definitive, to all practical purposes. Our people look upon this as different entirely.

Mr. MASON. The Senator will allow me to make an inquiry of him. I understood the Senator to say that there were powers conferred on these commissioners, by the act of 1850, which had not been conferred upon the judicial officers mentioned in the act of 1793.

Mr. COLLAMER. I did not say so.

Mr. MASON. Well, I understand the Senator to say that power is conferred on these commissioners to adjudicate. Now I ask the Senator, power to adjudicate what?

Mr. COLLAMER. Whether the man is a fugitive from labor or not.

Mr. MASON. The Constitution of the United States says that if a person held to labor or service in one State shall escape into another, he shall be delivered up upon the demand of the claimant.

Mr. COLLAMER. To whom the service is due.

Mr. MASON. Upon the demand of the claimant to whom the service is alleged to be due, or is due.

The requirement of the Constitution is, that if a person held to service escape, he shall be delivered up to that person to whom the service is due.

Mr. SEWARD. On claim.

Mr. MASON. He shall be delivered up, not to the person to whom the service is due, because that would lead to that inquiry; but he shall be delivered up to the claimant. Now, I would submit to the Senator this: what does the Constitution submit to the party who is to adjudicate? Does it submit anything more than the question, whether the alleged fugitive was held to service in the State from which he escaped? Does it submit an inquiry whether he was rightfully held to service, or does it submit the single question, was he held to service, whether rightfully or wrongfully, and did he escape? Having had something to do with the law of 1850, I aver that that law submits to the judicial authority that single inquiry: was he held to service? without inquiring whether he was rightfully or wrongfully held—was he held to service, and did he escape? If it is found that he was held to service, and did escape, the Constitution requires that he shall be delivered up, and the law says so. That is the whole of it.

Mr. COLLAMER. All that does not relieve the subject at all. The gentleman all the while seems to presume that no man can be taken up under that law, unless he is a runaway slave. That is an entire assumption. A man, and especially a colored man, in New England, who never was out of the State of Vermont, might be claimed as a slave and arrested and brought before a commissioner. Those are the people we are trying to protect, and those are the people we are bound to protect, and those are people whom our law is meant to protect. The gentleman from Virginia may state it as formally as he pleases; after all, has not the commissioner to decide this: was John Doe, now standing before me, *de facto*, if the gentleman pleases, not *de jure*—I do not make that point, but I am putting it on his own ground—bound to service, under the laws of Virginia, to the honorable Senator from Virginia? Were you, or were you not? that is the question. I do not say that the commissioner is to go into an inquiry of whether the law that bound him was good or not. That is not the point I am at; but when he is claimed to have run away from Texas as a fugitive slave, and he is brought before the commissioner, the question for the commissioner is, is this man a fugitive slave? and if he decides that he is, goes to Texas into slavery without any trial, unless you call that a trial. That is not a preparatory step; that is not ministerial; that is not introductory to some other proceeding; it is definitive, practically final.

Our people dislike this feature of the law. It submits to the commissioner the question as to identity of the man claimed, whether he is a man bound to service or not. I do not say he is to decide whether the man was rightfully or wrongfully bound to service; but I mean he is to decide whether he was the man that escaped—the fugitive—and if he is, what then? Are you to take him back, as you would a fugitive from justice, for a trial? Not at all. That is the trial, practically the only trial. Our people look upon that as a different thing. They did indeed provide, as the gentleman from Georgia charges, and I desire to turn attention to that. He complains, in the appendix to his speech, that

"Vermont pledges the whole power of the State to maintain the claim of the slaves to freedom."

No such thing. It does provide——

Mr. MASON. If the Senator will allow me to interrupt him—I will not unless it is agreeable to him—I wish this thing right as far as the law for the reclamation of fugitive slaves is concerned; and I do not see that there should be any difference between the honorable Senator and myself. The honorable Senator says now that I reason upon the law as if it was a law made to reclaim fugitive slaves, but that I do not reason upon it as if it might possibly be extended to one who was not a slave. Now, sir, the Constitution says nothing about slaves, nor does the law.

Mr. COLLAMER. I used the shortest term.

Mr. MASON. Very well. The law follows the Constitution. The Constitution says that

"No person held to service or labor in one State, under the laws thereof, escaping into another, shall, in consequence of any law or regulation therein, be discharged from such service or labor, but shall be delivered up on claim of the party to whom such service or labor may be due."

The law follows the Constitution. Its provisions are these, very briefly: upon the proofs to be adduced by the claimant, if it shall appear to the judicial officer in the State where the fugitive is arrested, that he was held to service or labor in the State from which he escaped, and that such service or labor was due to the claimant, he shall be delivered up on the faith of the Constitution—no inquiry whether that service or labor was rightfully or wrongfully due.

Now, the honorable Senator says that that is final; that it is not, as in the case of a fugitive from justice, preliminary only as to the guilt, but it is final. Final, how? Does that honorable Senator mean to intimate that there is a State of this Union where African bondage is recognized—and to one of those States this fugitive slave must be reconveyed—where the most ample, plenary, sedulous provision is not made to give every negro who is claimed as a slave the amplest opportunity, without fee or reward, to have the question tried there whether he is a slave or not? If that be true, the proceedings of the commissioner may be final or not, as the case may be. If the person is really a slave, when he is surrendered to his master, it is final. If he is not a slave, let him be taken wherever the sun shines upon a slave State, to make a complaint anywhere, in any village, at any cross-road, or on any highway, to the neighbors, that he is a freeman, and I will tell that honorable Senator, if he does not know it, that there would not be a voice in that whole community that would not insist upon his being remitted to all the privileges and securities which the law gives him—to a trial which is provided for at the public expense—to decide whether he be a slave or not. Those are the facts.

Mr. COLLAMER. I choose to make no issue with gentlemen from the slaveholding States in relation to the generosity, liberality, or anything of that kind, of their people. Indeed, I am free to acknowledge that I think they are generally quite as frank and liberal people as any, and I think they are great deal better than their institutions. Their institutions I regret; the goodness of the people I do not. I said that the commissioner's decision was final to all practical purposes. I know it is said the courts are open to him; and Dr. Johnson said, "so is the city coffee-house free to furnish a man with a good dinner, if he has the money." I said this step was not preliminary to any suit. I say so now. I can be easily understood in that, if you desire to understand me. When you enter a regular complaint against a man for a crime, and you send to another State to bring him, it is to bring him into court to answer to that offense charged against him in a proceeding already instituted and pending in a court. Then I say the order to return such a man, for such a purpose, is preliminary; but when you come to a fugitive from labor or service, is the action of the commissioner a step preliminary to anything of that kind? I do not say there could not be a suit brought afterwards by the man who is carried away as a slave to Texas——

Mr. MASON. I will not interrupt the Senator hereafter. If he will fasten that quarrel upon the Constitution, I will not defend the Constitution; but I insist upon the quarrel being fastened upon the Constitution, and not upon the law.

Mr. COLLAMER. Well, I do not choose to make that a point. I am not like the man who when the sermon did not please him, found fault with the text. I shall not find fault with the text any way. (Laughter.) Certain it is, then, that I am well founded in my distinction, that this is not a preliminary proceeding. It may be that the man can bring an action after he is carried away to Texas. I mention Texas simply because it is one of our most distant States. He is carried away to Texas, an entire stranger, and in utter poverty and destitution. Perhaps he could assert his rights there, but he would be much like the man getting his dinner at the city coffee house, if he had no money to buy it. The court being open does not assist him any. Besides he is not in a condition to go there. All his witnesses are in Vermont or Massachusetts where he was born.

The whole of these arguments go on the ground that gentlemen from the South really suppose, they have it at all times on their minds, that nobody else will be arrested but a fugitive. We are not safe that way, and our people have made some laws with a view to the security of their citizens on that account. They were not satisfied with leaving the question entirely to these commissioners, who, the Senator says, are judicial officers, but with no judicial powers in them; who are not subject to impeachment or trial. They were not satisfied with that condition of things. They did not like the law; but that was not all.

Another crisis came. Some time afterwards it was regularly decided by the Supreme Court that the descendant of an African negro was not entitled to any rights which white men were bound to respect at all. Suppose a man comes after a fugitive slave, as you choose to call him—perhaps one of your slave stealers in the southern States may come North, and steal easier there—he gets a description of the man, and gets affidavits in due form, comes into the New England States, or New York, and seizes a man answering that description; takes him to a commissioner, a stranger, and adduces his proof. How can we be safe? How can our people be secure against this; especially, I say, when it was holden, as I have stated, that he had no rights? Then it comes to this: if you come and get a fugitive slave, all very well; if you get a man that never was a fugitive slave at all, it is just as well, because he has no rights that you are bound to respect.

So we saw, from step to step, that there was no security for our colored population whatever, except what the State, in its almost utter imbecility, might give. Now, I can say, that whatever statutes have been passed, so far as my State is concerned, I believe were passed with no intention to avoid and break down this provision of the Constitution. They may run counter to it; they may look, upon their face, as if they were intended to defeat it; but our people always expect their laws to be subject to the Constitution. They expect that their own courts and the Supreme Court of the United States will set aside as void any law they make that contravenes any provision of the Constitution. They expect that, though they do not put in the words, "subject to the Constitution of the United States." (Laughter.) I may say further to gentlemen, that if there be any such statutes in Vermont as do contravene that provision, they will be as readily decided to be unconstitutional, I venture to declare, by the supreme court of that State as they would be by the Supreme Court of the United States.

I know, Mr. President, that our supreme court is chosen annually by the Legislature, but they make no distinction amongst parties. The present chief justice of that court has been upon that bench for twenty-three years, always a Democrat; a Democrat to begin with, and is now and always has been, and I am afraid always will be, for he recently published a letter in favor of the whole programme. His sentiments are well known. We expect our laws to be decided constitutional or unconstitutional by our own courts, and especially to abide by the decisions of the Supreme Court of the United States. We have no expectation of making any war on them. If it should happen that any of our laws are really unconstitutional, I hardly think that it lays the foundation of charging men with perjury and treason, and all the words of vituperation and invective that the English language can furnish, because we may happen to be mistaken.

Sir, when the State of Georgia passed a law, that a man who resided in the Indian territory in that State, by license of the President, and by consent of the nation, as a missionary for a long time, should not be allowed to remain there without license from their Governor, and made it finally a penitentiary offense if he did, they took a citizen of Vermont and imprisoned him in the penitentiary. The Supreme Court of the United States decided that law of theirs was unconstitutional. The gentleman (Mr. TOOMBS) says that, after all, the man did not get that certified, so that the court of Georgia did not disobey it. True it is, that man, with the other gentleman in the same position, was given very distinctly to understand that he could not get out of prison in that way, but that if he would cease his prosecution he might be pardoned; and as the only hope to get out they did cease, and they were pardoned. Now, sir, I do not think that the State of Georgia should have imputed to it any bad design or improper motives about that.

Mr. President, I cannot but here say, that, to my mind, the fact of a State passing unconstitutional laws, furnishes no foundation for what gentlemen claim. I deny that any State in this Union can lay the foundation for a dissolution of the Union by passing unconstitutional laws. The doctrine of the Senator from Georgia is, that if a State, or several States, pass laws contravening the Constitution of the United States, and which, if you please, are injurious to others; in that case the compact is broken, and the other States are at liberty to treat it as vacated whenever they please. I deny that doctrine. I deny, in the first place, that the States, as several States, entered into this compact. That, however, is repeated so often that, upon the whole, I do not know but it is believed. When a State acts, it acts in its organized capacity, by its organs, by its legislature, or by its Executive. There never was one of the States of this nation that acted in that way in the adoption of the present Constitution. The people of the United States, meeting in the conventions in their several States, adopted the United States Constitution. The States never acted on it as States. It would be a paradox that they should have done so. How could the Legislature of North Carolina, for instance, invested as it was, at that time, by the people with the power to levy and collect duties upon imports; how could the State, in its organized capacity, through that organ delegate that power to another body? It could not be done. It never was done. It never was attempted to be done. The people of the United States had to meet in their several States in their original condition, as people in convention, for these reasons: first, it was more convenient; next, if the people of North Carolina had invested their Legislature with the power to levy and collect duties, the people of North Carolina alone would have the power to invest that in another body; to wit, Congress. If you called the whole people of the United States, it would be a different set of people to take that power away from the one who gave it. No, sir, it is not true that this is in that sense a Confederacy. It is a national Government. I say it is a national Government, operating by its own act on individuals, and enforcing its own laws by its own executive power. The old Confederation was a failure. This is a national Government.

If these things be true, can it be possible that any State in this Union can dissolve it, or, if you please, lay a foundation for others to dissolve it, by passing unconstitutional laws? It is utterly destructive of the whole principle of this Government. There is no foundation for it at all. Then I deny that, because laws may have been passed, mistakenly if you please, that were unconstitutional, against the United States Constitution, that is any foundation for a dissolution of this Government. But there is another very strange thing in all these assertions; and that is, that upon a certain contingency, the election of a Republican President, the Union is to be dissolved on account of those laws. Pray, what relationship is there between them? It is pretty much like one man telling another, "If you had not caned me today for my insolence, I would have paid you that debt a month ago." (Laughter.)

The next point made upon us is, that it will not do to go on with the Republican party in possession of the Government, because gentlemen say we are going to break down the Supreme Court. There is another principle of our party mentioned in this connection, and that is, that we are going to exclude the South from the Territories. On this last point I have already said all that I wish to say. This is exactly what has been done from the beginning. It is the very thing the Government was made for. Now, in relation to breaking down the Supreme Court, I have but a few words to say.

I have always understood, as a lawyer, that the judgment of a court was binding upon the parties and privies—no more. It is binding upon the parties to the suit, and upon all who claim under them, who are privy to it. There it ends. The judgment of a court of competent jurisdiction is to be executed to that extent, and there it stops. The United States, I take it, were never a party to the Dred Scott decision, nor a privy to it in any legal sense. Then it has no binding force, as a judgment, on the United States. Should it have any force as a precedent or authority? It was a political decision as to the power of the Government to forbid slavery in the Territories. That is a question relating to the exercise of the political power of a coördinate branch of the Government. If that is not political, I do not know what is. Well, now, how has that always been viewed?

Some years since, the Supreme Court very deliberately decided that the Bank of the United States was constitutional. The Democratic platform, I believe, even in the last version, following its predecessors, contains an express resolution that it is unconstitutional. We see, then, how it is understood, by that party at any rate, that a decision of the Supreme Court on a point of that kind is good for nothing at all, unworthy of any respect, and that their own party decisions in their platform are of higher authority, more validity, and more binding. I do not choose to quarrel about that. It is a matter between them and the court. I take it, however, as authority, and it seems to me that, at any rate, gentlemen who stand upon that platform ought not to insist much on the decisions of the court.

But, Mr. President, the Dred Scott decision, as a precedent—and certainly that is its only effect on us in point of law—I take it, is neither infallible nor inscrutable. I hardly think any gentleman will stand here and say that he claims for the decision of the Supreme Court, as precedent and authority, that we should bow down to it as we would to the inscrutable dispensation of Divine Providence; or that we should even say blasphemously of it, "the Lord has given, the Lord has taken away; blessed be the name of the Lord." This will not be claimed, I apprehend. Then it is to be examined; and its worth as a precedent depends on the soundness of the arguments that sustain it and the principles on which it stands. If it has any weight, it is that; and, by the way, if the arguments are good to sustain the principle, they would be just as good without the decision of the Supreme Court as with it.

Now, Mr. President, I wish to examine this decision of the Supreme Court a little. They expend a great amount of time in undertaking to show that the power of the Government over the territory beyond the Mississippi, territory which was not owned at the adoption of the Constitution, does not arise and exist under the territorial clause of the Constitution—I mean the clause giving Congress power to make all needful rules and regulations. I care very little about that. I think it is totally unfounded in its reasons on that point, but I care very little about it for another reason. The court say that there is, after all, a power in this Government to obtain territory by conquest or treaty. They further say, that there must necessarily be, incident to that power and to the power to admit States, authority, when the Government has acquired a Territory, to frame a Government for it, so as to pass it through a condition of pupilage, and prepare it for admission as States. I care very little whether the power came from that clause or not; they say there is that power, any way; and they say that, in framing the laws for that purpose, it is in the discretion of Congress to make provision: it is not for the court to say what form of government they shall give it. They say further, that, the territory being a part of the United States, "the citizens enter it under authority of the Constitution, with their respective rights marked out and defined." But they say "this power is in the discretion of Congress," and that, of course, they are to frame the form of government in such a way as they believe will best advance the interests of the whole people.

They then spend some time discussing whether, in doing that, Congress can exercise any powers except some that are delegated expressly by the Constitution. I look upon all that part of the opinion as mere talk, because they say that the Constitution has not delegated to Congress any power to govern the territory obtained after the Constitution was adopted; that that is merely incidental to their power to obtain territory. Of course there is nothing in the Constitution by which it is said what the forms of power shall be that they shall exercise there. But they then come to talk about another topic. They say that Congress, in the exercise of power in the Territories, can do nothing that is expressly prohibited by the Constitution. Very well; let us take it so. They go on to enumerate a number of things that they say Congress cannot do. For instance: they cannot establish a religion, cannot abridge the freedom of speech or of the press, cannot abolish trial by jury, and so on, naming things that are expressly forbidden in the Constitution. Is it anywhere forbidden in the Constitution that Congress shall prohibit slaves being carried there? All the prohibitions they mention are express prohibitions. Is there such an express prohibition as that? How can you read into the Constitution a prohibition among those that are there, which is not there? That is what is attempted to be done. How do they get at it? In this way: they say, in the first place, that slaves are property, so recognized by the Constitution; in the second place, that everybody has a right to go to the Territories with every kind of property; and, in the third place, that to prohibit their doing so, is to violate the fifth amendment of the Constitution, which says that no person shall be deprived of life, liberty, or property, without due process of law.

In making up this syllogism, each proposition in it, whether major or minor, and the ultimate conclusion, are equally important. In the first place, then, are slaves property? The court utterly disregarded their own decisions on that subject in making this. I think if anything can be established from the decisions of courts it is that slavery exists by local law, confined to the territory over which the law is operative; and if persons held in slavery go out of and beyond that territory, they are no longer slaves; and if slaves are property by the law within that territory, they are not without it. In relation to this point, whether slaves are property beyond the States so recognizing them, I deny the major proposition, to begin with. I say the very language of the Constitution implies the contrary. It says that if a person holden to service under the laws of one State escape into another, he shall be returned. "Held to service!"—how? Under the laws of a State. "Held to service under the laws thereof," is the language.

When that man bound to service in one State escapes into another State, is he property there? Can the master go and take him there, and keep him there, and sell him there, and use him there? If he is like other property, and the Supreme Court says it is precisely the same as other property, all that would be true; but we know it is not. That provision of the Constitution declares all laws of other States that would release him from the service void; that is all. It contemplates that such laws might be passed, but says they shall not have that effect. It does not discharge him from the service in the State where he belongs, and only provides for the man being surrendered up and taken where he belongs, and where he owes the service. The Supreme Court of the United States, in the case of Prigg *vs.* Pennsylvania, decided the very same thing. They in so many words decided that slavery was a mere local matter; I will cite their very words:

"The state of slavery is deemed to be a mere municipal regulation, founded upon and limited to the range of territorial laws."—10 *Peters's Report*, page 611.

What did the Supreme Court do with that decision of theirs when they decided the Dred Scott case? Never said a word about it; utterly disregarded it; never even explained it; never qualified it at all. I hold in my hand the authorities, as collected in Burge's Commentaries on Colonial and Foreign Laws on the subject of the conflict of laws with regard to slavery. I will not read it at length, but here and there. I hold, first, that at common law, by which I mean the common law of England, slaves could not be holden at all. They never were holden lawfully in England. When the question arose, it was at once so decided in Sommersett's case. I know there had been an opinion given before that time, when a question arose in relation to their navigation act, whether, under the navigation act, slaves were merchandise. It was not decided by any suit, but an opinion being called for by the privy council, an opinion was given that they were, and therefore, foreigners could not carry on the slave trade with the British colonies; they wanted it all themselves. The board of trade with the King in council, had their negative on the colonial laws. They disagreed to them whenever the colonies attempted to pass laws against the slavery carried there under the Assiento contract, which the gentleman (Mr. Benjamin) well understands. It was a profitable business to the trade of England; and whenever the colonies attempted to get rid of it, they immediately interfered. By the colonial charter, the King in council, had a negative on the acts of the colonial Legislature. Sometimes they were negatived in that way; sometimes acts were passed effecting the same end. In short, they forced the slave trade and the holding of slaves on the colonies by statute. By their power to regulate trade, they forced it upon the colonies when it was always against the common law. Such was clearly the cause as laid down in the authorities as collected by Burge. They passed, from time to time, statutes to aid and encourage the trade. He says:

"Sir John Hawkins was the first Englishman who, in 1562, introduced the practice of buying or kidnapping negroes in Africa, and transporting and selling them for slaves in the West Indies. In 1620, a Dutch vessel carried a cargo of slaves from Africa to Virginia."

After that was the opinion under the navigation act. He says:

"The Legislature of Pennsylvania, when the British colony, passed, on the 17th of June, 1712, an act to prevent the importation of negroes and Indians into that province. It was disallowed by Great Britain, and accordingly repealed by an act of Queen Anne, on the 20th of February, 1713."

* * * * * * * * * * * * * * *

"In 1765, the Governor of Jamaica informed the Assembly of that island, that, consistently with his instructions, he could not give his assent to a bill, which had then been read twice, for limiting the importation of slaves into that colony. In 1774, the Jamaica Assembly attempted to prevent the further importation by an increase of duties thereon, and for this purpose passed two acts. The merchants of Bristol and Liverpool petitioned against their allowance. The board of trade made a report against them. The agent of Jamaica was heard against that report; but upon the recommendation of the privy council the acts were disallowed, and the disallowance was accompanied by an instruction to the Governor, dated the 28th of February, 1775, by which he was prohibited, 'upon pain of being removed from his government,' from giving his assent to any act by which the duties on the importation of slaves should be augmented."

The same author declares:

"Upon the disappearance of slavery in Europe, it commenced in America. The great Powers, England, France, Holland, Spain, and Portugal, some of whom boast of the freedom of their institutions, exerted all their energies and authority to introduce and maintain it in their colonies, by means of the African slave trade. Their resources were employed, and their subjects invited and encouraged to fill their colonies with slaves. We turn with disgust from the various expedients by which these States endeavored to secure to themselves the monopoly of this odious traffic, to the revenues which they derived from it, and to the remorseless perseverance with which England and France uniformly resisted every attempt on the part of their colonists to check its progress.

"To the existence of slavery in their colonies, the parent States gave the fullest and most active encouragement. Under the sanction of their laws and the decisions of their courts, slaves became property. But whilst they sanctioned, encouraged, and recognized the legality of slavery in their colonies, they denounced its existence in their possessions in Europe."

This was not peculiar to England, but extended to the other nations mentioned.

Mr. BENJAMIN. Will the Senator permit me a moment? I ask him just there, whether the author cites any authority showing that the English Government discouraged slavery in England at the time these colonies had it introduced among them—whether he cites a solitary authority or historian?

Mr. COLLAMER. I will read:

"There exists, then, a *status* which is legal in the countries in which it is constituted, but illegal in another country to which the person may resort.

"In this conflict there has been a uniformity of opinion among jurists, and of decision by judicial tribunals, in giving no effect to the *status*, however legal it may have been in the country in which the person was born, or in which he was previously domiciled, if it be not recognized by the law of his actual domicile.

"This principle was adopted by the supreme council of Mechlin as its established law. In 1881 it refused to issue a warrant to take up a person who had escaped from Spain, where he had been bought and legally held in slavery."

* * * * * * * * * * * * * * *

"Although the *Edits* of April, 1615, and May, 1685, had recognized the title to slaves and the legality of slavery in the colonies of France, yet within that kingdom it was illegal."

Mr. BENJAMIN. The Senator perhaps does not understand the precise question I put to him. If I understand him aright, he says that that author declares that, although the English Government established slavery, and forced slavery on its colonies on this continent, it discountenanced slavery at home, and slavery was not recognized at home.

Mr. COLLAMER. I did not say discountenanced.

Mr. BENJAMIN. Refused to acknowledge it.

Mr. COLLAMER. Certainly.

Mr. BENJAMIN. I ask for the authority for that.

Mr. COLLAMER. It is frequently the case in the world, that strength and power overcome right for the time being, until justice and the proper tribunals of justice are appealed to. That proves nothing. It is when the competent authorities are appealed to and a decision is made, that we begin to ascertain what is the law of the country. As to what the gentleman asks me, now I will read to him further from the same volume:

"In 1729, Sir P. York, then Attorney General and Mr. Talbot, the Solicitor General of England, gave their opinion, that a slave, by coming from the West Indies, either with or without his master, to Great Britain or Ireland, did not become free; and that his master's property or right in him was not thereby determined or varied."

That was not the decision of a court; it was the opinion of the Attorney and Solicitor General.

"This opinion was acted on. Slaves who had arrived in England from the British colonies were bought and sold publicly in the cities of London, Bristol, and Liverpool; and in the year 1771, when the negro Sommersett's case was decided, it was said there were at least fourteen thousand slaves in London."

That was without law. They got there, as the author states, by virtue of the opinion expressed by Sir Philip York, who had no judicial power whatever:

"The court of King's Bench in that case [Somersett] distinctly and expressly recognized the principle that the *status* of slavery 'was a municipal relation, an institution, therefore confined to certain places, and necessarily dropped by passage into a country where such municipal relation did not subsist. The negro, making choice of his habitation in England, had subjected himself to the penalties, and was therefore entitled to the protection of the laws.'

"A few years afterwards the case of Knight *vs.* Wedderburn was brought before the court of session, in Scotland. The master claimed Knight as a slave, but the court adopted the principle that slavery was not recognized by the laws of that kingdom, and was inconsistent with the principles thereof; that the regulations in Jamaica concerning slaves did not extend to that kingdom, and repelled the defender's claim to a perpetual service."

In a more recent case, Mr. Burge says:

"It has been applied when the person has placed himself beyond the limits of the country in which the *status* existed by law, and became subject to the law of mother country whose institutions did not recognize that *status* though he did not put his foot on her shores."

That was where he went on board ship, and the ship carried him off. I also cite in the second Barnewall & Cresswell, decided by Chief Justice Best, where the whole subject is very fully examined, and where the same decision as in the case of Sommersett was made. I next cite not merely that case, but cases decided by the Supreme Court of the United States. I have already alluded to Prigg *vs.* Pennsylvania. There is also the case of Groves *vs.* Slaughter. That was a case from the State of Mississippi. Mississippi had forbidden the bringing of slaves there for sale; but if they were personal property, as the Supreme Court say in the Dred Scott case, the same as other personal property, the States could not regulate the trade in chattels of any kind between them. I take it, if slaves be property at all, they are personal property; for the Constitution says they are persons, and you say they are property. The States have no power to regulate trade between each other. The Supreme Court of the United States were appealed to on that subject, and it was insisted that the power was vested in Congress to regulate trade between the other States and the State of Mississippi, and that no State can forbid the sale of the property of another State within its territory. The Supreme Court, however, sustained the right of Mississippi to do what she did, clearly because slaves were not like other personal property. The States, the court said, had the right to prohibit such sale. In a case in Kentucky, Rankin *vs.* Lydia, in second Marshall, the words of the court are:

"We view this (slavery) as a right existing by positive law, of a municipal character, without foundation in the law of nature, or in the unwritten common law."

I do not wish to elaborate this point any more.

Mr. MALLORY. Will my friend from Vermont permit me to draw his attention to a single point? I perceive that he has quoted from the Sommersett case, and it has been referred to a great deal on the other side of the Chamber. I have not a very distinct recollection of it, but I will ask him whether, in that case, which is regarded here as a leading one, the sole question before the court of King's Bench was not as to the right of any man to take another one out of the realm of England without his authority or the authority of law; and whether the principle that a slave brought from the West Indies ceased to be a slave because he was brought to England was mooted there at all?

Mr. COLLAMER. The gentleman seems to have put together in his mind the case of the slave Grace, which was before Lord Stowell, and the Somersett case, that was before Lord Mansfield. The Somersett case was clear and distinct enough. The fact was, if the slave was the man's property, he had a right to take him. So the Supreme Court decided in the Prigg case, no distinction of that kind can be made. He had a right to take him away if he was property, but the court, in Somersett's case, held he was free in England. It is true that, in the case of the slave Grace, before Lord Stowell, a question arose as to what would be the effect of returning voluntarily into the master's service in the State where the service was due, after the slave had been brought out, and had been in England or France. Lord Stowell said that, if the servant Grace returned with her master, voluntarily, to her former *status*, she would be a slave still in Jamaica. I think that was the decision. That has been quite a mooted question here. Our Supreme Court, I believe, decided that in the Kentucky case of Graham *vs.* Strader; and if the Supreme Court, in the Dred Scott case, had simply confined itself to the fact that Dred Scott, wherever he was, voluntarily went back with his master to Missouri, and thereby returned to his former *status*, no man would ever have made a word about the decision at all.

There is another nice distinction about that made by Lord Stowell, and made, also, in a case in Pickering, in Massachusetts; and that is, as to whether the State or country into which the man goes, forbids slavery absolutely, or whether it only forbids the master from using power, as a master, over him there. If it is the latter, and he voluntarily returns, he waives that; but, if it is the former, and the slavery is declared absolutely void and ended, then the return would not affect it. That is, however, a nice distinction, which it is not necessary now to make.

The next point in the syllogism is, that slaves, being property like any other property, their owners have a right to go to the Territories with them. What is that founded on? I have no doubt that slaves are not property, though, perhaps, they may be called such where slavery is authorized by law; but even if they were, how does this follow? What is the reason that the slaveholder has a right to take his slave there? You say the territory which we have acquired belongs to the people of the several States. That is not true. It belongs to the people of the United States. If it belongs to the people of the several States, each several State would have its right to a proportion of it; and if it was sold by the General Government, they would have a right to their proportion of the money. Clearly so, if the General Government holds it as a mere trustee for the States, as *cestui que* trusts. Now, how idle is that. Here you hear one day that we own the territory, and that every man has a right to go there with his property, because each man has his share in the land; and the next day we admit it as a free State, and there is not a quarter of the land sold. Now, according to this doctrine, the people of the slaveholding States have lost all their land there. It is a most palpable inconsistency. The assumption that the several States have an interest in the land there, is not true. The whole theory of it is founded on a wrong doctrine.

In the next place, it is said that, inasmuch as slaves are property, and recognized as property by the Constitution of the United States, (which argument I have already answered,) if we do not allow the owners to go there with them, it is an infringement of their rights, and a breach of the fifth section of the amendments of the Constitution, which declares that no man shall be deprived of life, liberty, or property, without due process of law. It is a curious fact, that the extremes of this question seem to meet on this common ground. One man says we cannot permit slaves to exists in a Territory at all. Why? Because, he says, we cannot deprive any man of his life, liberty, or property, without due process of law. Now, if you permit slaves to be holden in a Territory, you deprive a man of his liberty. I say you do not. I do not understand that when they allowed slavery to continue to exist in Louisiana, they deprived any man on earth of his liberty. It was gone before. So, too, when they allowed slaves to be taken, as they did, into Mississippi from Georgia, did they deprive any man of his liberty? No; he was deprived of it before. So the opposite extreme of the question cite not only the Constitution to support their doctrine, that you cannot prohibit slavery in the Territories, but cite the very same words. They say you cannot prohibit it, because it will deprive the owner of his property. The others say you cannot allow it, because it will deprive somebody of his liberty.

The fact is, neither is well founded. When the Missouri compromise line was made, there was not a white inhabitant, or black inhabitant, in all the vast uninhabited region, north of that line—not a settler in it. When the line was run, and it was provided that no slavery should be admitted north of it, I want to know if there was a slaveholder in the United States that parted with any of his slaves? Was there a slaveholder in the United States whose slaves were confiscated? Was there a slaveholder in the United States whose slaves were set free? How, then, can you say that the adoption of the Missouri compromise line confiscated any one's property; or, in other words, deprived a man of his property without due process of law? It did not deprive any man of his property at all, with or without process of law. You have laws in your own States—Virginia has one, and, I think, Maryland; most of the slave States—against bringing in blacks, and especially slaves, for sale; they forbid it. Does that confiscate any of the property of the slaveholders of Maryland, or of any other State? Not at all. Does it deprive any man of his property? Certainly not at all.

I have stated all there is in the Dred Scott decision. The only reason given in the world, the only one suggested, why Congress cannot forbid the taking of slaves into the Territories, is because it would infringe that article of the Constitution, and deprive some man of his property without due process of law. It is a mere assumption, totally unfounded; for, when the act was made, it did not deprive any man of his property, and could not, and never could.

Mr. President, when we consider that this court have utterly disregarded their own decisions, have made assumptions on which they have founded their opinions, which are thus utterly inconsistent; when we examine this decision in the light any of us possess, I say it is not entitled to respect, even as a precedent; and further, in all this there is no intention to break down the Supreme Court. They have disregarded their own decisions in making this. I take it they will disregard this when they come to make another. They have certainly the power of revision.

And now, Mr. President, I will bring my remarks to a termination. The whole question is, in effect: shall we restore the compromise line by excluding slavery from the territories? Is not that peace? Was it not peace while it existed? Is not this the olive branch? Is it not the harbinger of repose? Is it wrong? Is it outrageous? Is it any violence? It is simply to bring back things to where they were; and all I can now say is, that if the Republican party is true to its purposes, and can effect them, it will effect that peace, even to the South—for I do not believe they ever asked for that repeal, or ever wanted it. I believe it was altogether the exertion of politicians and a scramble for the Presidency. If anybody, by that repeal and that Kansas-Nebraska bill, shall ever get to be President by virtue of it, and succeed in the purposes for which it was entered upon, I am inclined to think that so far from being a cure, it will only add another evil to come out of this box of Pandora.

www.ingramcontent.com/pod-product-compliance
Lightning Source LLC
LaVergne TN
LVHW011145110826
845150LV00008B/2511
* 9 7 8 1 4 1 8 1 9 1 9 1 7 *